The Caribou
Feed Our Soul

Ɂétthén bet'à dághíddá

Fifth House Ltd.
A Fitzhenry & Whiteside Company
195 Allstate Parkway
Markham, Ontario L3R 4T8
1-800-387-9776
www.fifthhousepublishers.ca

CANADIAN NORTH
seriously northern

CIBC

Parks   Parcs
Canada Canada

Northwest
Territories Education, Culture and Employment

FSC
Mixed Sources
Product group from well-managed
forests and other controlled sources
www.fsc.org Cert no. SW-COC-1271
© 1996 Forest Stewardship Council

Cover and interior design by John Luckhurst
Photography by Tessa Macintosh
Additional photographs by Wayne Lynch (page 9 caribou, 10, caribou, hare, and muskoxen); John A. Nagy, GNWT (pages 10 and 11, aerial image of caribou migrating; page 13, caribou; page 25, caribou); Native Press, 1971 (page 19, Indian Brotherhood); NWT Archives/Fumoleau/N-1995-002:10290 (pages 20-21, Old Lady of the Falls); René Fumoleau (page 22, Beaver Lodge).

Series editorial by Meaghan Craven

The type in this book is set in 10-on-15-point Trebuchet Regular and 10-on-13-point Tekton Oblique.

Fifth House Ltd. acknowledges with thanks The Canada Council for the Arts and Ontario Arts Council for their support of our publishing program. We also acknowledge the financial support of the Government of Canada through the Book Publishing Industry Development Program (BPIDP).

The author would like to thank CIBC, WWF-Canada, Parks Canada, and Canadian North for financial assistance in the completion of this book.

Printed in Canada by Friesens on Forest Stewardship Council (FSC) Approved paper

2010 / 1

Library and Archives Canada Cataloguing in Publication

Enzoe, Pete
The caribou feed our soul / Pete Enzoe and Mindy Willett; photographs by Tessa Macintosh.

(The land is our storybook ; 6)
Ages 8 and up.
ISBN 978-1-897252-67-3

1. Enzoe, Pete—Juvenile literature. 2. Caribou hunting—Northwest Territories—Juvenile literature. 3. Chipewyan Indians—Hunting—Northwest Territories—Juvenile literature. 4. Lutsel K'e Dene First Nation—Biography—Juvenile literature. I. Willett, Mindy, 1968- II. Macintosh, Tessa, 1952- III. Title. IV. Series: Land is our storybook; 6

QL737.U55E59 2010   j639'.11658097193   C2010-904579-3

Dene often decorate their clothing with a fringe of caribou or moose hide.

Acknowledgements

We've been working on *The Caribou Feed Our Soul* for several years. Our chief concern was that readers understand the importance of the caribou to northern people, especially during the present times of population decline. As Pete has said many times, he feels it is one of his responsibilities in life to help protect the caribou. We therefore first want to thank you—the reader—for attempting to understand why people harvest an animal that is so important to the Denésołiné. We hope this book helps you on that journey of opening your mind to other ways of knowing.

There are many people who helped us along the way, but we would especially like to thank: Madeline Drybones for sharing so much of her skills and knowledge, and Miranda Casaway and Diya Drybones for working on the hides with Madeline while translating her stories; Pierre Catholique for his extensive knowledge of history of Thaidene Nene; Pete's sister, Gloria, for her passion about her culture and her words of wisdom that helped guide this book; Gloria's husband, Barry Shearing, and their three boys, Kohlman, Cameron, and Levi, for their delightful participation; Pete's other nephews, Kyle Enzoe and Dillon Enzoe, who are already able harvesters; and Pete's entire family, who have been very supportive of this book in many ways.

We would also like to thank: Chief Antoine Michele and his council for agreeing to include the very sacred story of the Old Lady of the Falls and encouraging the sharing of traditional knowledge with children; Celine Marlow and James Lockhart, the culture and language teachers at the Łutsël K'é Dene School; Shelagh Cavanagh, the school principal, and all the students who made us feel welcome; Jake Basil and Troy Catholique for helping with the harvest and sharing their snowsnake talents; JC Catholique for lending us his drum and helping to translate; Bertha Catholique for translations; Ray Griffith, Gordon Hamre, and Steve Elis for helpful advice; Brenda Hans, John Stewart, and Ms. Barb Prevedello and her Grade 4 class at the York School in Toronto, for all their editing and reviewing; and, of course, Meaghan Craven, our editor, and John Luckhurst, our designer, for their dedication to excellence and understanding of the need to take the time to get it right.

Tessa would like to acknowledge with gratitude the encouragement of her parents, Elizabeth and Macgregor Macintosh, who even in their 81st year continue to bring guidance, joy, and richness to her life. And thanks to her friend, Mindy, for her patience and persistence, both.

Mindy would personally like to thank her dear friend, John Laird, who initiated the funding that made this book series possible, as well as her husband, Damian, and their two children, Jack and Rae, who are the joy of her life.

For Levi, my nephew.
Learn to respect other
people and be a good
person in life.
— Uncle Pete.

The Caribou
Feed Our Soul

Ɂétthén bet'á dághíddá

By
PETE ENZOE
and
MINDY WILLETT
Photographs by
Tessa Macintosh

FIFTH
HOUSE

Great Bear Lake

Arctic Circle

Yukon
Territory

Northwest
Territories

Nunavut

British
Columbia

Fort Chipewyan

Brocket

Turnor Lake

Labrador and Newfoundland

Alberta

Manitoba

Quebec

Saskatchewan

Ontario

Prince Edward I.

New
Brunswick

Nova Scot

Nunavut

Gameti

Behchoko

Northwest
Territories

Yellowknife

N'Dilo   Dettah

Rat Lodge   Artillery Lake

Old Lady of the Falls

Beaver Lodge

Fort Reliance
(Desneth Che)

Mackenzie River

Łutsël K'é

Great Slave Lake
(Túcho)

Fort Resolution
(Deninu Kue)

○ Akaitcho communities

★ Pete's hometown

● Chipewyan communities
   outside the NWT

◆ Sacred sites

⬭ Beverly and Qamanirjuac
   caribou range

⬭ Bathurst caribou range

▢ Perimetre of the large
   regional map

Pete's mother, Liza, made him this caribou hide jacket.

ʔedlá net'é ʔá

I am the son of Philip and Liza Enzoe. I am *Denésǫłiné* (Chipewyan) from the community of Łutsël K'é, Northwest Territories.

Me, I stayed a lot with my grandfather, Abele Nitah, when I was growing up. He used to tell me lots of stories about why and how animals got their shapes and about how our land was formed. These were our bedtime stories. I used to love listening to those Old Time stories.

I still love those stories, and I like to tell them to my nephews. Even though things have changed, they've stayed the same, too. We used to use dogs to travel around. Now we use snow-machines. But how I feel about the land hasn't changed. Me, I love the land and all that it provides; especially caribou. Caribou are everything to us.

I'm going to tell you about how we came to be here, about what caribou mean to us and our life today.

Pete Enzoe

Pete's nephew, Cameron, proudly stands in front of his community sign.

WELCOME TO LUTSEL K'E DENE FIRST NATION TRADITIONAL TERRITORY

I was born at Old Fort Reliance. There aren't any people there anymore, just old log cabins. I now live in Łutsël K'é, the most northern Chipewyan community. My town name comes from a small fish called a *łutsël*. I know it's hard to say but Łutsël K'é (Thloot-sel-kay) rhymes with "It's okay!" Give it a try!

2

Territory

There is no road to and from Łutsël K'é. To get there you can fly, use a snow-machine, or take a boat. There are about 320 people in Łutsël K'é. It has a nursing station, a Kindergarten to Grade 12 school, and a CO-OP grocery store.

Łutsël K'é is one of five Akaitcho territory communities. Akaitcho is the name of our traditional area, and it is quite large because my people were nomadic and used the land all around Great Slave Lake, which is called Túcho in my language.

The territory was named after Akaitcho, a famous leader. In 1821 he rescued the explorer John Franklin while he was on his first Arctic expedition. In 1825, after many years of war, Akaitcho made peace between his people and the Tłı̨chǫ. In 1900 my people also made an agreement of peace and friendship with the Government of Canada.

My parents had 10 children. I am the second eldest. Me, I don't have a wife or children, but I help take care of many nephews and nieces and try to teach them what they need to know. I tell them to be respectful of their elders; to watch what skilled people do; to trap, hunt, and fish. I've also taken lots of school kids out on the land to give them important skills, like ice fishing.

Pete teaches his nephew, Dillon, how to set and check traps for martin. Setting a trap properly ensures that an animal dies instantly and does not suffer.

Pete sets a net under the ice using a jigger, such as the one shown here. He checks the net every day. To find out more about jiggers, go to page 24.

When I was about 13 my parents let me go out on my own in the bush. I had a dog with me so I had no problem. I wasn't scared. I walked away from town and stayed out for a few days. I had to get my own food. I had some moose sinew, so it was easy to snare a rabbit.

The month was June, and I had no tent. There were lots of mosquitoes, so I burned lichen on a rock and that kept the mosquitoes away. It felt good to be on my own. When I came home, my parents were happy. They knew I was ready to be a man. Nowadays, not too many kids do that; that's too bad.

Here, Uncle Pete and Kohlman have pulled a few whitefish, Pete's favourite, from the net.

Pete shares some meat and laughter with his nephew, Kyle. They spend many hours on the land together, hunting, fishing, and trapping. Because Pete is always laughing, people call him Nadló, which means "laughs a lot."

5

Us, when we're out fishing or hunting on the land, we play games, like hand games (dá ?udzí). To play, two teams of people take turns hiding objects in their hands. One team hides the objects and the other team tries to guess which hand they're in. Sticks keep score. We use a loud drum and lots of movement to try to fool the other team.

Pete and James Lockhart, the cultural language teacher at the school, play hand games with some students in a canvas tent.

My grandfather taught me many other games. He once made me a caribou bone game called *k'éguwí*. It is a stick attached to a string of hide. On the end of the hide string are several hollow caribou toe bones. There is also a piece of hide that has holes in it. To play, you have to try to get the bones onto the stick or the stick into the holes of the caribou hide. The more bones you pile onto the stick, the more points you get. You need a lot of patience to do it well.

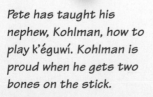

Pete's grandfather also taught him how to use a snowsnake (yáth ká hékóth). Troy, Dillon, and Jake make snowsnakes from straight spruce trees. They make their snakes smooth and pointed at one end. Then, they throw their snowsnakes across the surface of the snow to see whose goes the farthest.

Pete has taught his nephew, Kohlman, how to play k'éguwí. Kohlman is proud when he gets two bones on the stick.

7

Out on the land, there are no distractions like TV. It's quiet and peaceful. You can really hear the animals, especially in springtime. When the chores are being done, or when we're relaxing after a game or a meal, there's always time to share stories.

Dillon and Jake get fresh lake water in front of Pete's cabin.

Inside Pete's cabin, Dillon and Jake dry out their boot liners. The cabin is on Ganyon Lake. It is about 75 km south of Łutsël K'é. Pete sometimes takes a few students here to teach them land skills.

Our stories tell us that we
Denésoliné are descendants of
the caribou. We call caribou *Ɂétthén*
in our language, and we also use the
word *Ɂétthén* for stars. We believe
caribou come from the stars. My
grandfather told me they come
down from the stars on the northern
lights (*ká nagís*, "they move in the
sky"), so I know that when I see the
northern lights there will be caribou
in the area. This makes me happy
because caribou are our main
source of food.

The caribou we harvest go north to the tundra to calve in the spring. They return to us in the late fall, when we start to see stars in the sky after the long summer of no darkness.

For the last few years there haven't been many caribou around. This has happened before, and it is natural. Sometimes there are none; sometimes there are many. When there aren't that many, my people rely on other food. These past few years we've had to go far to hunt—all the way to the tundra. I've hardly taken any caribou. I'm mostly eating moose and muskoxen and hare. This is one way we can make sure there will still be caribou for our grandchildren.

The snowhoe hare, or ʔá, help sustain people when caribou are scarce.

Several caribou herds migrate near Pete's home, including the Bathurst, Beverly, and Qamanirjuaq herds. Check out their ranges on the map on page vi.

Our Words

dątśą — *raven*
deníye — *moose*
ʔá — *snowshoe hare*
ʔétthén — *caribou*
ká nagís — *northern lights*
łutsël — small, white fish found near Łutsël K'é
yuthę ʔere — *muskoxen*

There are many muskoxen living just north of where Pete lives.

I work with scientists to monitor the herds and to count the numbers of individuals and determine if they are bulls or cows. I also attend many meetings to pay attention to what companies want to do on our land. While it is important for people to have jobs, we must first take care of the caribou and the land.

Migrating caribou at a water crossing on the tundra.

Pete counts caribou from a helicopter to get a population estimate.

Pete and biologist Damian Panayi discuss the data they have collected on caribou before heading into meetings in Yellowknife, the capital city of the Northwest Territories.

I want caribou to always be here. I see one of my roles in life as a protector of caribou. I do this in many ways. I've been paying attention, listening to my Elders and learning from them since I was a small boy. I've learned the caribou trails and their ways. I go on the land as much as possible and think about what the caribou are doing. I share this knowledge with others.

Pete takes a group of students hunting. He stops at a high point of land to describe the ridges and lakes, and to talk about how caribou travel.

Pete shows Dillon which way two caribou are travelling. By the size of the tracks, he knows one of the caribou is a female and the other is her calf from last spring.

Caribou hoofs are large and wide like snowshoes.

Moose, deer, and caribou all belong to the same family, but unlike the others, both male and female caribou have antlers at certain times of year. Females are usually smaller than males.

Caribou like to sleep on the lake, away from the trees. This way, they have more time to notice wolves coming, and then it's easier to run away. During the daytime they go into the bush to eat lichen. When it's windy, caribou will be on the lake, even during the day, because they can't smell predators when the wind is up.

13

When the caribou come, it is a sign that they are giving themselves to us. If we need meat, then we harvest them. When we hunt, we give thanks for the life given. We try to use every part of the caribou. I bring the hides and meat to my auntie, Madeline, who will use them to make beautiful clothes and drymeat.

Pete explains to Dillon how to properly and respectfully butcher a caribou so that nothing is wasted.

Pete removes a caribou hide and will give it to his Auntie Madeline.

Our Stories

How Raven Became Black

Told by Pete Enzoe

There is a story for every animal. Sometimes I forget what my grandfather told me, but, somehow, when I see an animal or am walking through the bush it's like his stories come back to me. He once told me about Raven. Raven used to be all white. You know how ravens are always yacking away, making noise. They've always been like that. Well, one time one of the other animals, he got tired of Raven yapping away, so he put ashes all over him to make him quiet. Ravens have been black ever since then.

Whwhen we harvest a caribou we make a fire and enjoy a meal of fresh roasted meat before heading back to town. We'll bring the best pieces of meat back to the Elders.

Pete and Dillon feed the fire a piece of caribou meat to give thanks to the caribou.

Auntie Madeline Drybones is my mom's sister. She spent most of her life on the land. She's very strong and used to hunt and trap with her dogs. She has lots of skills and passes her knowledge on to her grandchildren. Her husband, Noel, passed away, and she now mostly stays in town. I bring her fresh meat, which she cuts and makes into drymeat, and hides, which she prepares to use later for making clothing.

Sometimes Madeline leaves the hair on caribou hides so she can make caribou blankets.

The first step in tanning hides is to remove the hair and scrape them until all flesh is removed.

Madeline soaks the scraped hides in a solution of caribou brain and water for a couple of hours. This will make them soft and pliable.

Madeline washes the hides to remove remaining blood and then squeezes them to remove excess water.

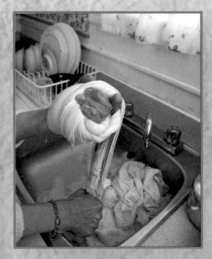

Madeline's granddaughter, Miranda Casaway, cuts up meat to make drymeat.

Hides can be left white or they can be smoked until they are a tan colour. Pete's sister, Gloria, sewed a vest for her son Levi's Kindergarten graduation from a smoked hide she got from Auntie Madeline.

Madeline hangs the hides on the line outside where the sun can bleach them. She places small pieces of wood between the hides to keep them from sticking together. The hides are taken down when they feel dry like paper.

We know that the best way to make sure caribou are here forever is to take care of our land. The people of Łutsël K'é have worked hard to keep our land healthy. We have not allowed mining companies to drill for uranium here, because we are worried it will poison the water and land. We are also working with Parks Canada to try and protect large areas from development. We have chosen to call the new park Thaidene Nene, which means The Land of Our Ancestors.

Thaidene Nene includes spectacular cliffs, the deep waters of Great Slave Lake, and both taiga and tundra. The background on the next page shows the beautiful patterns and colours in the rock from the east arm of Great Slave Lake.

Pete talks to his sister, Gloria, and points to his trapline on a map. Gloria works for the Łutsël K'é band on the plans for the new park. Aboriginal harvesting rights have been guaranteed in the park.

My community didn't always want a national park. Pierre Catholique was chief in 1969 when government people asked him to sign over our land for a park. There was a meeting with many government people. Chief Catholique refused to sign because our people had not been consulted. He said, "Never again will one chief sit down with many government people." Later that same year the Indian Brotherhood was formed.

Pierre Catholique now supports the national park. He says the Dene people are in charge and that good jobs will come to his community. He believes that Thaidene Nene will help keep the land healthy.

The Indian Brotherhood

Although life was harsh, the Dene had independence before the Europeans came to the North. During the 19th and 20th centuries, Europeans thought their way of life was better than that of the Dene, and they did many things to take away their freedom. Government and churches took children and put them in residential schools, people were forced to move into communities, and natural resources were taken from the land without permission. By 1969 the Dene had had enough and formed a group called the Indian Brotherhood. The Brotherhood worked to uphold the rights of the Dene. In 1978 the Indian Brotherhood's name changed to Dene Nation.

The Indian Brotherhood in 1971.

Our Stories

The Legend of *Ts'qkuí Thédá*
(The Old Lady of the Falls)

Told by Madeline Drybones
Translated by Diya Drybones and Pete Enzoe

There are many special places within Thaidene Nene. My auntie, Madeline, grew up near *Ts'ăkui Thédá* or "The Old Lady of the Falls," which is in her backyard. This is a sacred place to us. Our stories have been told in many ways, but this is the version my auntie told me.

Madeline Drybones

Madeline and her granddaughter, Diya, share stories while stretching a caribou hide.

Along, long time ago there was a medicine man whose name was Xáchogh. He was big. He was chasing beavers because the people were starving. The beavers had a lodge at Artillery Lake (Ɂedáchogh tué). All the islands in Artillery Lake come from the air bubbles of all those giant beavers. That beaver lodge is still there to this day and when people pass through there to go caribou hunting they make an offering at that place. The beaver lodge was chopped on one side by Xáchogh, which is why it looks the way it does.

Xáchogh, he got one small beaver, but the others got away, and he chased them all the way down the Mackenzie. The places where he chased the beavers are marked. You can see where he shot an arrow, and where the beaver bled, it is all red. That one beaver he got was large, though, and the people ate the meat right away.

One lady, she wanted some of the beaver blood, but Xáchogh couldn't give her any because there wasn't any left. She was mad and said, "I'll wait here until you bring me some." Xáchogh and the other people left to go chasing after the other beavers, but the lady stayed where she was, waiting for Xáchogh to return. She was waiting a long time so she got stuck in the river. When the people went back they found her stuck there.

She's still in the river waiting. It's a sacred place. To this day people go there to heal themselves. There are two pools, the bowls in which she holds water, at the bottom of her dress. That's where people go to be healed by her. Many people have been healed when they go and pray to her. If you have cancer you can go there to get healed, but you shouldn't share your stories of your experience, it might backfire. Don't tell anyone.

The old lady also provides food for the people. She uses an awl and pokes under the arm of a caribou or other animal and it floats down the river to the people. One time we found a moose like that, just after the Elders told us that story. A moose came floating by—the meat was still good, and when we scraped the hide, that's what we found: a hole under the arm.

I am keeping the land, the caribou, and my people's stories and traditions alive and healthy for my nieces and nephews.

Pete always makes an offering when he stops at Beaver Lodge.

Pete's nephew, Kohlman, in the clean water of Túcho.

I have spent my life on the land of my ancestors. I will continue to share the stories of my people, and I will continue to read the land as I travel.

All the Details!

Akaitcho Territory – includes the Yellowknives and Chipewyan First Nations peoples who today live in the communities of Ndilo, Dettah, Fort Resolution, and Łutsël K'é. They claim an area of 480,000 km² of traditional lands to the north, east, and south of Great Slave Lake.

Denésǫliné – The Chipewyan refer to themselves as Denésǫliné (pronounced Den-a-sooth-leh-na), which means "human beings." They are part of the Athapaskan language group and their language has official status, in the Northwest Territories. There are approximately 11,000 Chipewyan living in the Northwest Territories, Manitoba, and northern Alberta and Saskatchewan. The name *Chipewyan* comes from the Cree name for this people, meaning "pointed skin," after the design of their jackets.

Ɂedáchogh túe – Artillery Lake.

Ɂétthén - stars and caribou.

hand games – challenging games to understand but really fun to watch. Go to www.denegames.ca or search for "Denhandgames" to watch some of the many videos.

Ɂedlá net'é Ɂá – How are you?

jigger – a tool used to set a net under ice. First you chisel or auger a hole in the ice. Then, you put the jigger, with a rope attached, into the hole. When you pull the rope, a lever on the jigger raises up, and when you release the rope, the lever springs back. You move the jigger along under the ice, with the up and down motion of the lever "grabbing" the ice and creeping forward, stringing out the rope for the length of your fish net. You can follow the jigger's progress by listening for it through the ice or, if the ice is clear, watching it move along. When the jigger has made its journey, you make another hole in the ice to retrieve it and pull the end of the rope out of the water. Now, you can use this rope to thread your fish net.

ká nagís - northern lights.

k'éguwí - caribou bone game.

land claim – an agreement that is recognized in the Canadian constitution between an Aboriginal group and the government of Canada. The Akaitcho are negotiating their agreement but have not yet signed it.

lichen – the most important plant caribou eat. It is made up of two living things (fungus and alga) that can only survive when together.

Nadló - "one who laughs a lot"; Pete's nickname.

population estimate – the best, educated guess about how many individuals there are in a group of living things at a given time. A new population estimate is always compared to the last population estimate. The change between two estimates is important. A decline (or decrease) in numbers could mean the species is in trouble.

taiga – the northern part of the boreal forest where coniferous trees still grow but are smaller and spread out compared to the southern parts of the boreal forest.

Thaidene Nene – is the name of a proposed national park on Łutsël K'é Dene land. Łutsël K'é Dene First Nation (LKDFN) are worried about companies wanting to mine and otherwise develop land. The LKDFN is working with Parks Canada on a plan to share the responsibility of the management of Thaidene Nene with the hope that it will bring economic benefit to the community while maintaining the health of the land.

Tłįchǫ – The Tłįchǫ, formerly known as the Dogribs, are also Dene and their language is related to that of the Denésǫliné.

treaty - a formal agreement between an Aboriginal people and the government of Canada. Today treaties are called land claims. The Akaitcho are part of Treaty 8, which was signed in July of 1900 in Fort Resolution.

Túcho - (*Tu* – lake, *cho* – big) Denésǫłiné name for Great Slave Lake.

tundra - the land north of the taiga, where it is generally treeless.

Xáchogh – a hero known by different names in each Dene group. The stories told of how he made the land safe (such as getting rid of the giant animals) tie the Dene people to the land and to each other. He is one of the most important cultural leaders and gave all Dene people their laws.

yáth ká hékóth - snowsnake.

Caribou Quick Facts

Caribou are mammals and are part of the deer family. They are ungulates, which means they have hoofs. All caribou are members of the same genus and species, and their scientific name is *Rangifer tarandus*. The wild caribou in Canada are either woodland caribou or barren-ground caribou. The woodland caribou are the larger of the two and are found south of the Arctic Circle. The caribou shown on the Canadian quarter is a woodland caribou. The type of caribou that live near Pete are barren-ground caribou, and they migrate long distances.

To learn more about caribou and listen to how they sound, go to: http://www.taiga.net/projectcaribou/

Caribou Adaptations to the Cold

Short, thick muzzle (nose and mouth)—warms cold incoming air, which keeps heat and moisture in

Small body, tail, and ears—the less skin the better! A lot of heat is lost through skin

Hollow, insulating guard hairs

Thick, crinkly, protective underfur

Large, wide hoofs are like snowshoes

About the Authors and Photographer

Pete Enzoe is *Denésoliné* from Łutsël K'é, Northwest Territories, which is on the east arm of Great Slave Lake. He is a hunter, fisher, and trapper. He sees his role in life as protector of the caribou and spends much of his time reading the land as he travels his people's traditional areas. He shares his knowledge with young people.

Mindy Willett is an educator from Yellowknife, NWT. *The Caribou Feed Our Soul* is the sixth book she has co-authored in *The Land is Our Storybook* series. When not writing she can be found paddling or skiing on the other side of Great Slave Lake from Pete. Once while out skiing she even bumped into him as he was snow-machining to Yellowknife from Łutsël K'é.

Tessa Macintosh is an award-winning northern photographer who raised her family in Yellowknife. In 35 years she has been fortunate to photograph many wonderful northerners and fantastic places across the North. Tessa loves to float a canoe on Great Slave Lake as the full heat of the long summer sun builds. This is to prepare for the cracking solid -35-degree winter nights filled with dancing aurora.